SAINT MARY'S
IN THE
MOUNTAINS
NEVADA'S BONANZA CHURCH

December 9, 1997
To Bill and Virgina
Broersma - With
Best Wishes
Virgil Buchanan

NEVADA'S BONANZA CHURCH
SAINT MARY'S
in the
MOUNTAINS

The history of Virginia City's
Saint Mary's In the Mountains
Fully illustrated with historic photographs
of the Comstock Lode

by Virgil A. Bucchianeri

Gold Hill Publishing Company
Gold Hill, Nevada

The number of this book is designated on the Daughters of Charity School library marker found in a book belonging to T.F. McCarthy, an Irish Miner and Parishioner during the boom days on the Comstock.

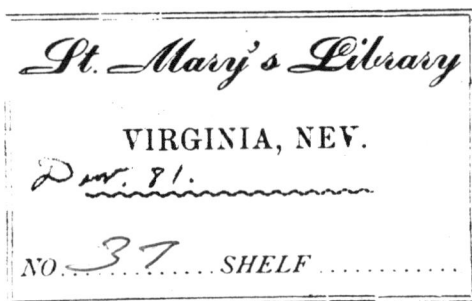

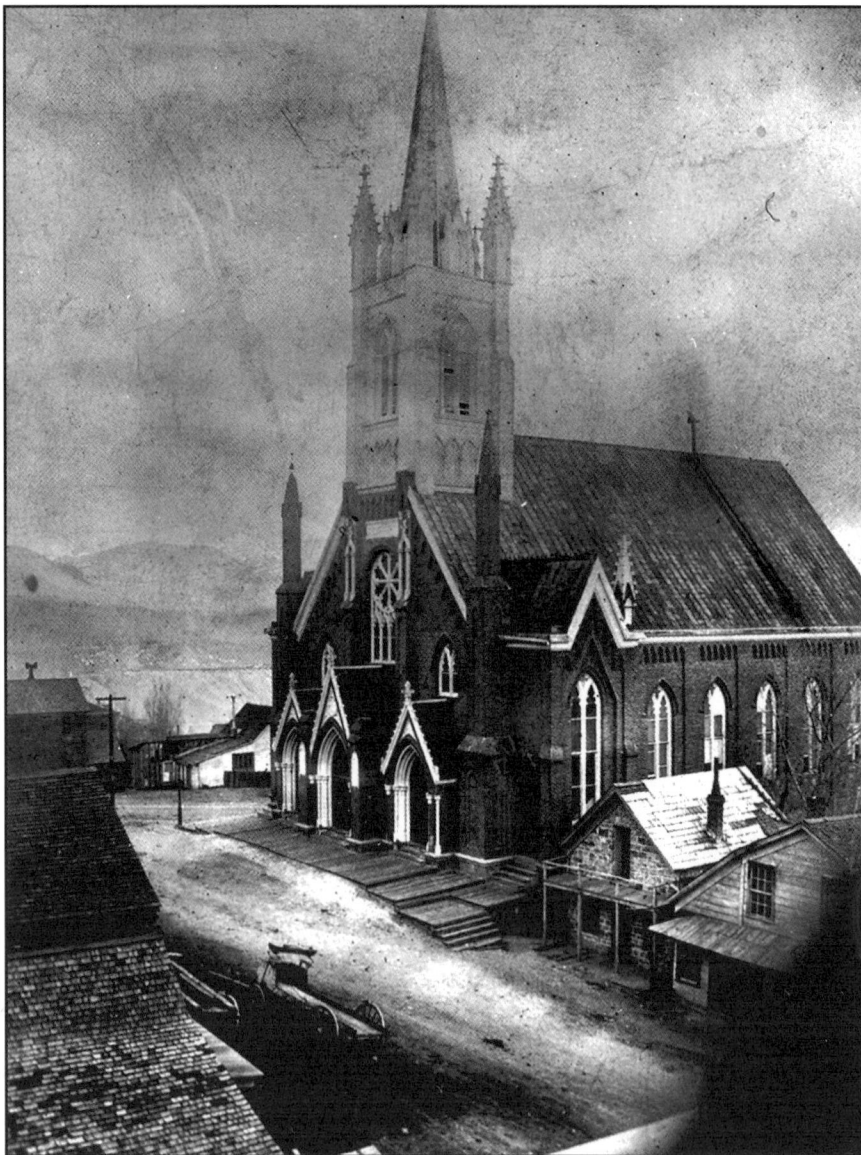

St. Mary's in the Mountains in the 1880s.

Table of Contents

St. Mary's in the Mountains as it appeared shortly after the dedication in 1877.

Prologue

CATHOLIC FAMILY ALMANAC OF 1882 (T.F. CcCARTHY ESTATE)

St. Patrick, Apostle of Ireland

Ode to the Irish Miner

There's a mountain in Nevada
Where the Shamrocks cannot grow
Where the Leprechauns hid their treasure
Three thousand feet below

But O'Reilly and McLaughlin
With a bit of Irish luck
and "Old Virginia" Finney
Stumbled in the muck

They found the buried treasure
and in Eire the tale was told
and a thousand eager Irishmen
arrived to dig for gold

The West has many heroes
Courageous, Brave and Grand
But the great Bonanza Kings
All came from Ireland

And back among the Shamrocks
The Leprechauns still say
That they up and lost their treasure
on a mountain far away

Courtesy: Irish Miner at the Delta Gift Shop

Father Bernard Michalik is the present pastor of St. Mary's (1997). He will be celebrating his Golden Jubilee in the priesthood in June 1997 and is held in great affection by his parishioners as a true "mountain shepherd."

Virgil Bucchianeri, the author, maintains an office and home in the "Old Mooney" house, across from St. Mary's. He served four terms as Storey County District Attorney and is presently in private practice.

David W. Toll, the publisher, is the author of several books and numerous newspaper articles on Nevada and the West, including The *Complete Nevada Traveler*. He was publisher and chief editor of the late, great Gold Hill News, and resides in the tumble-down remnants of the Gold Hill mansion belonging to his great-great uncle, John P. Jones, U.S. Senator from Nevada for thirty years.

Message from Bishop Phillip F. Straling
Bishop of the Diocese of Reno

Easter 1997

Dear Friends:

Catholic teaching understands the Church to be the people of God, the Catholic community with Christ as its head. Needing a place to gather to pray and celebrate the Sacred Mysteries, buildings are constructed to house the community called a church or sanctuary. The building takes on a sacredness of its own because of the Catholic community which gathers there. It is the place where the Catholic Community celebrates Mass, Eucharist, and other Sacraments. It is a place of prayer, a place to celebrate important events in our lives such as the baptism of a child, a marriage or the burial of a loved one. The church also becomes sacred because, as Jesus said, "Where two or three are gathered together, there am I in their midst."

So the building of St. Mary in the Mountains is not just another building, but a very special and "sacred" one. On this location, buildings have stood and stand today serving as a sign of the life and work of the Catholic community in Virginia City. In a world that all too often forgets about God, this structure stands as a reminder that there are men and women of faith here.

As we approach the year 2000, St. Mary in the Mountains is unique in that it represents a continuous Catholic community in Virginia City and Nevada since the 1850s. It continues to be the place of worship and welcomes many visitors and peoples of all faiths. May those who attend services or visit this church feel the sacredness of this place. May attending liturgy or saying a prayer in this church draw us closer together as brothers and sisters, help us to experience the presence of God, and receive His blessings and peace.

By this reprinting of "St. Mary in the Mountains–Nevada's Bonanza Church," we give thanks to God and to all who have been a part of this community of St. Mary in the Mountains.

Sincerely Yours in Christ,

Most Reverend Phillip F. Straling
Bishop, Diocese of Reno

AUTHOR'S NOTATION: Bishop Straling has used the proper name as carried on Diocesan records of "*St. Mary in the Mountains.*" I have followed the older possessive form commonly in use among the people of The Comstock — "*St. Mary's in the Mountains.*" —V.B.

"The Mountain Shepherd"

"The mountain messenger is ever welcome to speak about the mountains, the glens, and the valleys, the rushing streams and the Paiutes, the Washoes and Shoshones, the murmuring brooks and warbling songsters, the snows, the forests and refreshing breezes.

"In this light…I can very well stand before you. For more than twenty years I have been roaming over the vast and arid plains of Nevada… The villager, the miner, the rancher and mountaineer were my constant companions… The mountain shepherd in the midst of wild scenery, is rarely unhappy in his pastoral duties… the beauties of nature are dim reflections of the perfections of God…"

Commencement address by Bishop Patrick Manogue to the graduating class of St. Mary's College at the Grand Opera House, San Francisco, May 31, 1883.

Comstock Prayer

If when we've done with earthly strife
There be a Paradise or Sheol
Or any other named abode
Which we may gain through love or pity,
Grant me a heavenly Comstock Lode,
A spiritual Virginia City.

Joseph T. Goodman
Editor, Territorial Enterprise
1861–1874

Acknowledgments
& Dedication

Most of the information related came from newspapers published at the time the events occurred. Additional sources not otherwise cited in the text include excerpts from *Comstock Bonanza* by Duncan Emerich, *Condemned to the Mines, the Life of Bishop Eugene O'Connell,* by Msgr. John T. Dwyer, *History of St. Mary's* by Sister Frederick Ann Hehr as published in the *Territorial Enterprise,* and *Seventy Five Years of Catholic Life in Nevada,* by Bishop Thomas K. Gorman. Many thanks are due to Father Bernard Michalik, present pastor of St. Mary's, as well as Bishop Phillip Straling for their moral and financial support. The first printing published in 1986 has long been sold out, and it was through the support of Father Michalik and Bishop Straling that this second printing has been made possible. Again, I thank David Toll and the personnel of Gold Hill Publishing for bringing the book into print.

This second printing is dedicated to the memories of Father Charles Bengel, who made possible the first printing, and to Fathers Daniel Keelan and Sam Tambourin, who passed away during their tenures as Pastors of St. Mary's. In an age when St. Mary's could no longer be rebuilt, I hope, as did Father Bouchard, the dedicatory speaker, that it will endure as long as the mountains which surround it.

Virgil A. Bucchianeri
Virginia City, Nevada
1997

BOB RICHARDS'
TOURIST OF THE WEEK

"But why did they build such a big church for such a small town?"

A view of the interior, showing the choir loft and balconies, and the mission cross taken to St. Mary's from the Gold Hill Parish of St. Patrick's in 1918.

Preface

Virginia City is a tourist Mecca for those seeking the remains of the Old West. It has always been and is now a town known for its free-spirited Wild West ways. In its heyday, over 110 saloons catered to the thirsty miners, and today with a population of less than 600 people, over 20 of these establishments still line the old wooden sidewalks. In 1859, it was the site of one of the most important gold and silver discoveries in the world, and thereafter, miners flocked to the region, the majority from Ireland, to work the miles of underground tunnels.

In seeming contradiction, the most famous landmark of all dominates the town and immediately catches the eye of the approaching motorist—the spire of St.. Mary's in the Mountains towering over the old mining town—for as the Irish miners toiled in the mines and relieve their hardships in the saloons, they also erected their monument to the Faith that had been long suppressed in their native land. When the Bonanza discoveries faded into the history books, it became the surviving glory of the Comstock Lode. Today, the church is visited by a constant flow of tourists of all creeds and nationalities. The *Territorial Enterprise* stated in 1957 that generations of Nevadans not necessarily of the Catholic faith had made it everybody's church and that it belonged to the community as a whole.

It is not an old church by European standards, but in 1876, it was rebuilt in the style of an old world cathedral, modified to fit "modern purposes," as a contemporary newspaper put it, so that even without its historic past, it is a beautiful church. Anything over 100 years old is historic in the American West, however, and the church stands today as the most significant monument in the most famous mining town of the Western frontier.

Father Manogue at the Yellow Jacket Mine Fire in Gold Hill, Nevada, on April 7, 1869. Taken from the "Big Bonanza" by Dan de Quille, 1877

I
The Early Catholic Churches

The first Catholic church was built in Virginia City in the summer of 1860 by Father Hugh P. Gallagher. Father Gallagher had arrived in the West via the Isthmus of Nicaragua in 1853 and followed his brother, Father Joseph Gallagher, to the Comstock after the silver discoveries of 1859. This first church collapsed during a heavy wind in the following winter. He did not remain long in the area, building a church in Carson City, which suffered the same fate, and another in Genoa, which was purchased shortly thereafter as a courthouse.

In 1862, Father Patrick Manogue arrived on the Comstock and began construction on the first St. Mary's, a wooden edifice located a block South of the present church. The Irish miners placed "Manogue's Kitties" in all the saloons of the city for donations to the building funds. By August 21, 1863, *The Virginia Evening Bulletin* was able to report that the steeple was nearing completion. On September 18, 1963, a benefit netted $5,814,55. Dan de Quille reported the affair when he was finally able to locate a counter in a far corner which dispensed alcoholic beverages, from which he could view the event. By September 21, 1863, the church was being used for services, and the "stirring tones of the huge bell warns

Father Hugh Gallagher, a native of Killy-Gordon, Ireland, Builder of the first church in Virginia city in 1860.

us three times every day of the rapid flight of time, ringing at 6 a.m., 12 noon and 6 p.m., being of great assistance to those who work outside without time pieces," reported the *Bulletin*. A huge benefit was held on St. Patrick's day of 1864, with a parade of five military companies, a High mass, and a grand ball at Maguire's Opera House.

Meanwhile, a wooden structure was also built to the Southwest, on the "Divide" between Gold Hill and Virginia City, by Italian Passionist Fathers, who had arrived on the Comstock in September 1863. By December 1863, their church, known as the Immaculate Conception, was completed. In May 1864, another Irish Parish, St. Patrick's, was established in Gold Hill. Jurisdictional disputes arose over the performance of marriages and baptisms, and a tactical error was made by the Passionists when they criticized the Irish Bishop Eugene O'Connell, who had jurisdiction over the Comstock and had sided with the Irish parishes. The Passionists closed their church and were moved to Mexico by their Provincial in September 1865.

On July 17, 1864, the first St. Mary's was dedicated by Bishop O'Connell, with the assistance of the Italian Passionist Fathers, who were still on the Comstock. This first St. Marys was completed at a cost of $12,000 and remained in use through October 1870. Mozart's *Twelfth Mass* was performed with full choir and orchestra there on Christmas day 1869, and visitors stated that it had seldom been performed better in the East. It was still existing in 1871, when a fire almost burned it down, starting in wooden savings from a carpenter's bench, but this church ceased to be used when the rapidly increasing population necessitated the building of a larger church.

The Comstock in 1861, showing the first cemetery to the west on Scorpion Hill (I) and Father Gallagher's short-lived church (II).

II
Patrick Manogue—
Miner, Priest, Bishop

The memory of Patrick Manogue is emblazoned on a large marble block high over the front of St. Mary's, and on a metal plaque by the front door. He was born in County Kilkenny, Ireland on March 15, 1831. He joined the California Gold Rush in 1854, working in the mines at Moore's Flat, in the Mother Lode. He saved enough money working as a miner for a seminary education in Paris, France, where he studied at the seminary of St. Sulspice. He was ordained a priest by Cardinal Morlot, a few days before Christmas of 1861; he arrived in Virginia City in June of 1862, answering the call for more priests by Bishop Eugene O'Connell, bishop of the old Grass Valley diocese, which included most of the rough and desolate Territory of Nevada.

Manogue traveled the entire Territory of Nevada ministering to his flock. On one occasion, he retraced a trip of 180 miles through a blizzard to secure a reprieve for a condemned man from Territorial Governor Nye, after he had been called to administer the last rites prior to his execution. He was on hand on April 7, 1869, at a great fire in the Yellow Jacket mine in Gold Hill, where 36 miners died in the underground shafts. Being of gigantic build, he intervened to save Charles Bonner, a Comstock mine superintendent, from being hanged by 2000 striking miners after Bonner had attempted to enforce an order from his employers lowing the daily wage from $4.00 to $3.50. Manogue reportedly hid Bonner in the church belfry for three days and then got him out of town to safety in San Francisco. Manogue had also become known for wresting a gun from a brutal husband who tried to prevent his wife from receiving the last rites during a terminal illness.

Alfred Doten, Comstock newspaper editor, records that he was a congenial man, however, as in a diary entry for December 13, 1865, Doten states that he visited Manogue with Dan de Quille, a reporter for the *Territorial Enterprise* and associate of Mark Twain on that newspaper. "Father Manogue, Father O'Reilly, and another Father, together with Dan de Quille and myself consumed two bottles of champagne and lots of whiskey, and all had a jolly time," he wrote.

Father Manogue was one of the few priests who was never moved from his parish by Bishop O'Connell, and he ultimately succeeded in building the church that stands today as one of the last surviving glories of the Comstock Lode. For nearly twenty years, he labored as a parish priest in Virginia City, and on January 16,

1881, he was consecrated Bishop at St. Mary's Cathedral in San Francisco as co-adjutor of the Grass Valley Diocese. He died as the first Bishop of Sacramento on February 27, 1895, leaving instructions to be buried in a simple priest's plot, and not in the Cathedral he had built in Sacramento, as had been planned.

Father Patrick Manogue in a formal pose taken in Virginia City. He was described as an Irishman of "gigantic stature," being 6'3" tall and weighing 250 pounds.

III

The First Brick Church

••

On July 24, 1868, a site had been cleared of frame buildings for the first brick church. By August 14, 1868, the Virginia City brick factory of Kerrin & Company had completed a specially built $50,000 kiln, to be fired by $2,000 worth of cord wood, the firing of the kiln being set for Sunday, August 16, 1868. A second kiln was added as the basement builder, a Mr. O'Neil, was making rapid progress with his portion of the work. 350,000 bricks were to be used in the walls and steeple.

On August 18, 1868, an impressive cornerstone laying ceremony was held, with Bishop O'Connell carried in a canopy by four men from the wooden church one block to the south. Eight Daughters of Charity, who had arrived on the Comstock in 1864 to operate a school and orphanage, accompanied Father Manogue at the head of the procession, followed by the Metropolitan Brass Band. Two hundred members of the St. Vincent de Paul Society and the congregation, as well as the children of the school and orphanage, marched in the procession. The cornerstone itself was four feet long, three feet deep, with a tin box containing coins, records of the church society of St. Vincent de Paul, newspapers and other items. Presumably this stone is still in place some-where behind the front porch of the church, although the exact location has been lost.

The work languished through 1869 and most of 1870, as Father Manogue would only proceed as he had funding on hand, and reportedly ran out of funds on at least two occasions. Though the roof was almost completed and the brickwork of the spire was underway by November 12, 1868, the spire was not completed until September 2, 1870, measuring 157 feet, 6 inches from the ground to the top of the cross. It was also not until September 1870, that substantial work was done on the interior, being finished up in plaster and wood carvings of white and gold gilt coloring.

The altar, imported from France, was of a "marble-like" composition, as reported by the *Territorial Enterprise,* and of a plaster composition as reported by the *Gold Hill News.* It arrived in 480 pieces on September 28, 1870. It was completed on October 13, 1870, sitting on a below-ground foundation, and weighing 6,700 pounds, being 21 feet tall. The altar was fronted with figures of the Twelve Apostles, carved pillars and scrolls, and was of Gothic style.

On October 23, 1870, Mass was said

for the first time in this church. The Emmet Guard, an Irish military company, appeared in full uniform and presented arms at the elevation of the Host. This impressive edifice was to last but a short five years, the interior and roof being gutted in the great fire of 1875. When the smoke had cleared, the greater portion of the exterior walls as well as its famous "Silver Bell" had survived the fire.

A rare view of the pre-fire brick church taken in the early 1870s. The basement, made of stone, and part of the walls survived the Great Fire of 1875. Also visible is Father Manogue's first wooden church in the process of being closed out, as the steeple has been removed. The photograph was given to Father Paul Meinecke, pastor from 1963 to 1974, by railroad historian Stephen Drew after a long search to find a photograph of the church as it appeared before the fire.

In 1874, the Missionary Father Patrick Hennebery advocated temperance among the Irish miners at St. Mary's. He died in 1897 and is buried in Virginia City.

By 1865, Virginia City had grown into a populated area, with most buildings built close together and constructed of wood. On St. Patrick's Day of 1864, Maguire's Opera House (I) was the scene of a huge fund-raising effort for the first wooden St. Mary's (II), situated between the Episcopal and Methodist churches. It is easy to see how fires could sweep through the town. On November 25, 1867, Father Manogue officiated at the wedding of John Mackay, future Bonanza King, to Mary Louise Bryant, a widow who took in washing for the miners. As Mrs. Mackay, she subsequently became one of the wealthiest women in the world, spending most of her time in the high society of Paris. Her departure for Europe caused her husband to spend much of his time on the Comstock in a suite of rooms in the Gould & Curry Mine office, now called "The Mackay Mansion." This marriage was given special notice in the Territorial Enterprise, as the staff had been given a case of Krug champagne in honor of the event. The brick church would be built in the center of this photograph.

IV

Saint Mary's Silver Bell

• •

The first brick church, with Frank Thayer, architect, Thomas Cordiell in charge of construction, and Tim Cronin as the bricklayer finally neared completion in September, 1870. The spire of the church had been completed by September 2, and the following day a large bell arrived aboard the cars of the recently-completed transcontinental railroad in Reno, from the Meneely Bell Foundry of West Troy, New York. The bell was the largest "between the Sierra Nevada Mountains and the Missouri River," according to the local papers, and weighed 2,264 lbs. with a 100 lb. clapper. The frame weighed "about as much." The bell was hauled up the Virginia City by teams as the Virginia & Truckee Railroad had not yet been completed to Reno. The bell arrived at the church six days later, on September 8, 1870. It was found

THE
Meneely Bell Foundery.

Established at West Troy,
N. Y., in 1826.

Post Office Address, either Troy, or
West Troy, N. Y.

This well-known establishment created the reputation of TROY CHURCH BELLS, and has sustained the same by a production exceeding that of all the other founderies in the country combined. One thousand testimonials received during the last six years. All Bells warranted. New Patent Rotary Mountings. Illustrated Catalogue sent free.

E. A. & G. R. MENEELY, West Troy, N. Y.

An advertisement for the Meneely Bell Foundry, published in 1873 in the Catholic Family Almanac.

that the trap doors of the steeple would have to be enlarged before the bell could be installed. Another month was to go by, but finally the bell was suspended in place by October 7, 1870. Father Manogue insisted that the bell not be rung until the church was completed and formally opened. The *Territorial Enterprise* reported that, "were we Father Manogue, we'd ring her one clatter now—just for luck." It remained silent, however, until the formal opening of the church, and on October 23, 1870, at six o'clock in the morning, it range out for the first time, over "the happy land of the sagebrush."

Newspapers of the time reported that the bill was made of the "finest bell metal." An encyclopedia of the period states that "bell metal" is made of a composition of copper and tin, and that silver if used in any quantity would injure the tone of a larger bell. Nevertheless, the story persists that St. Mary's has a bell made of Comstock silver. The story is not without some substance, however, as Rev. Thomas Tubman, who served as assistant pastor from 1884 stated that a Mr. Lynch, a generous benefactor of the church, brought a quantity of Comstock silver to the East to be included in the bell. The story evolved over that years, so that an article in a local newspaper in the 1960's stated that the bell was of solid silver cast in Spain from bullion from the

Lady Bryan mine. It was not cast in Spain, nor is it of solid silver. It is certain, however, that this same bell survived the Great Fire of October 1875, and is the same bell which hangs in St. Mary's to this day, continuing to ring over the "happy land of sagebrush." One of the old altar consecration bells or gongs, as well as the altar crucifix appears to have a silver coating, and it is very possible that the Comstock silver was used on these items, where it would be visible to the congregation.

The Belfry of the present-day St. Mary's in the Mountains, houses the bell that arrived on the Comstock in 1870. The bell (inset), survived the Great Fire of 1875, when its fall was broken by the trap doors of the belfry. It lay on its side, partly buried in the ground until it could be re-hung in the rebuilt church. Also visible is the large marble block designating the name of the church and boldly proclaiming Father Manogue as its pastor. A similar block with a Latin inscription survived the Great Fire but was subsequently broken by workmen during reconstruction, so that they suffered the wrath of Father Manogue's Irish temper.

V
The Great Fire of 1875

On October 26, 1875, at 5:30 in the morning, a fire from a kerosene lamp started in a one-story rooming house on 'A' Street, high above the central portion of the city. A strong wind blowing from the west carried flying embers down onto the rooftops below. The steeple of St. Mary's caught fire, and was allowed to burn down to appoint where it could be reached by a fire pumper. At this point the fire equipment left the scene, as the fire seemed to be under control At 10:15 in the morning, however, another ember caught the roof on fire, and the equipment

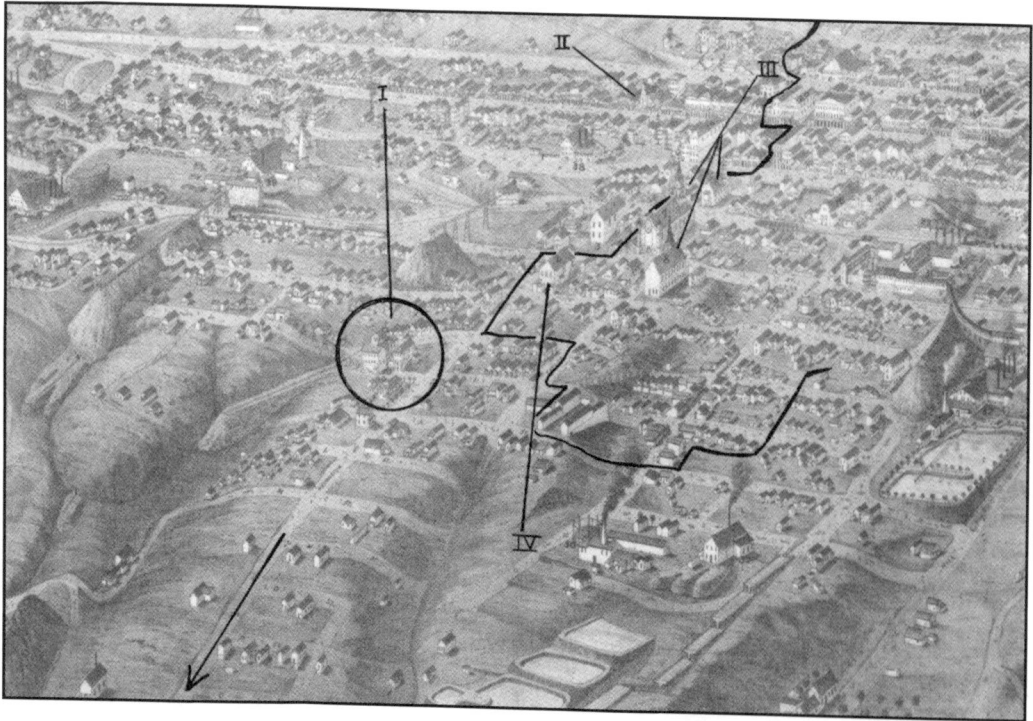

A map showing the lines of the fire of October 26, 1875, in the vicinity of St. Mary's in the Mountains. A strong wind, coupled with fire equipment having to give priority to saving the mine shafts caused a great loss to the businesses and residences of the city. The Daughters of Charity school and orphanage (I) and the Presbyterian Church (II) escaped the fire, as well as the Daughters of Charity hospital beyond the arrow in the lower left. Succumbing to the flames were St. Mary's, St. Paul's Episcopal church and the Methodist church (all shown at III). The public school (IV) was the site of the first wooden St. Mary's church, in use from 1863 to 1870.

could not be called back. Statues imported from France and other interior fixtures had been taken out, but the ornate French altar and a newly-built pipe organ could not be removed, and before long the fire had consumed most of the interior.

Through the years, the story developed that the church had been dynamited as a fire break at the request of John Mackay in an effort to save the nearby Consolidated Virginia mine, but in fact most of the walls survived the fire and were used in the subsequent reconstruction. When the smoke cleared, most of the heart of the city, and three of its churches had been destroyed. St. Mary's stood "blackened, empty, and desolate, like the wreck around it…" reported the *Gold Hill News*. Fortunately, the school and hospital operated by the Daughters of Charity had survived the fire, and services were removed to a new three-story brick building at the school on 'H' Street.

Forty to fifty trains a day arrived in Virginia City for the next several months with materials to rebuild the stricken city. Reconstruction on Saint Mary's though, was not a project that was immediately undertaken. In July, 1876, Father Manogue left for a trip to Oregon, with still no visible signs of reconstruction. He returned August 8, 1876, describing the Oregon climate as "delightful, with frequent showers in the vicinity of Mt. Shasta…"

A new and more imposing church, reflecting the optimism of the people about the future of the Comstock Lode, would be built using the old walls. Most of the exterior work was completed in a two-month period late in 1876. Damage was estimated at $60,000 and insurance proceeds covered half the cost of reconstruction. The Comstock economy had reached its peak at this time, and unknown to the people of Virginia City, the last of the Great Bonanza discoveries had been made. Thus the reconstructed church has stood for more than a century as a monument to the glorious times that preceded it.

"Making People Good…"

"When the fire reached the group of churches on Taylor Street, everybody was in a frenzy, grown-ups as well as children. I learned then that it took something more than belonging to a church to make people good. When the first of the three churches began to burn, men and women belonging to the other two seemed as happy as I was. They didn't think the fire was going to go any further. When it took a sudden leap and enfolded the second church, only the people belonging to the third were happy. The third church was almost all brick, and everybody thought it was safe, but it wasn't. Soon the flames began to creep up the steeple, which was wood and burned beautifully, and then, of all the watchers around me, only the children were happy. All churches looked alike to us, especially when on fire…"

—Reminiscences of a Virginia City childhood by John Taylor Waldorf in A Kid on the Comstock.

VI
The Church is Rebuilt

On September 16, 1875, the *Territorial Enterprise* reported that "the greater portion of the old walls stood in as good a condition as when first erected," and that "all parts at all shaken were being torn down." By October 4, 1876 "something of the intended make of the church could be seen." By November 15, 1876, the church tower again pointed toward heaven, with the cross 170 feet above the ground, making the spire 12 feet 6 inches taller than previously. On November 24, 1876, it was reported that the old bell had been removed to the interior, ready to be re-hung. "It seems to have incurred no injury by reason of having passed through the fire," reported the *Territorial Enterprise*.

On November 30, 1876, the *Enterprise* stated that "the new metallic roof appeared like a silver lake in the moonlight, with an intervening turret like a dark ship riding at anchor." To guard against future fires, a water pipe was installed which extended clear to the top of the steeple cross, so that the entire roof could be sprayed with water—a forerunner of our modern sprinkler systems. Father Manogue stated that this system could be used throughout the city and predicted its wide-spread use in future times. This water system was first tested on July 16, 1877, sending sprays of water over the roof and onto the adjoining streets. On July 26, 1877, the papers reported that red-

wood pews were being installed in the interior and that the wooden sacristy built over the east end of the church had been completed, but that the scaffolding was still up as it still had to be painted. The paper went on to say that the basement plumbing was also underway. The walls had been previously laid on heavy metal plates to minimize earthquake damage, and new tall redwood columns in the interior held the roof so that it could sway independently of the walls in the event of high winds.

To this day, the roof has a distinct loud creaking sound whenever a high wind, known locally as a "Washoe Zephyr" descends on the Comstock. Plans were made to plaster the outside walls to match the white steeple, but this never materialized.

The interior had an ornate wood Gothic altar, surrounded by a rich Brussels carpet and a choir loft and galleries built a third of the way down each side. The church was brilliantly lighted by a large gas chandelier, with gas jets in the form of blue and gold lilies on each redwood column. The ceiling was painted a sky blue, interspersed with gold stars, which reportedly gave a striking effect in the dim light of the roof area, the columns appearing to extend up to heaven. Needlepoint pictures laboriously may by the Daughters of Charity and copies of Old World paintings were hung throughout the church. Two side altars matched the main altar, and in the front entrance were placed two marble angels holding holy water fonts. A large baptismal font graced the interior, and a painting depicting the visit of Mary and Joseph to Elizabeth in the hills of Judea, as described in the gospel according to St. Luke, was placed high over the main altar, as it was in commemoration of this event that the church had been named St. Mary's in the Mountains. The papers reported that the building was a credit to the city and to the state of Nevada, and hoped it would not suffer the same fate as its predecessor. This is the structure that stands today.

Reconstruction of St. Mary's in the Mountains in 1876-77 (I), and the Daughters of Charity school and orphanage (II), as seen from the Combination mine shaft each of Virginia City.

Reconstruction of St. Mary's steeple and roof as seen through the stacks of the Consolidated Virginia works where four Irish "Bonanza Kings" uncovered the "Big Bonanza" of 1873. The newly rebuilt St. Paul's Episcopal church stands directly behind St. Mary's.

The Baptismal Font of St. Mary's in the Mountains. It is believed to date back to 1870, being one of the fixtures removed from the church during the Great Fire of 1875.

Virginia City in 1869, showing the first St. Mary's (I) and the new brick church under construction (II), taken from the site of the future Daughters of Charity Hospital. (Bancroft Library, University of California).

The painting of Mary in the mountains of Judea, by Felix Alcan, a Canadian painter, for which event the church was named, and which has hung above the main altar from the time of its 1877 dedication.

"Thereupon Mary set out, proceeding in haste into the hill country to a town of Judah where she entered Zachariah's house and greeted Elizabeth…"

—Luke: 1:39

17

VII
Opening and Dedication

By August 7, 1977, the church was in use, as the *Virginia Evening Chronicle* reported that Bishop O'Connell had preached there on the previous Sunday. On September 14th, the paper reported an incident that has recurred continuously into modern times. St. Mary's has always been located in the immediate vicinity of the public schools, and it was reported that on September 13th, a dozen boys arranged themselves opposite the church and whiled away the weary lunch hour by throwing rocks at the stained-glass windows, breaking three panes. "This practice should be stopped by arresting a few of the principal offenders and locking them in jail for a while," said the paper. To this day, the church remains such a temptation, and pastors periodically make the trek to the school principal's office to see if other lunch hour entertainments can be devised.

Despite this slight setback, the church was formally dedicated on Sunday, September 16, 1877. The pews, made of redwood with white pine moldings, were filled to capacity. At 7 o'clock in the morning, Bishop O'Connell, assisted by pastors including Father Manogue and Father Hugh Gallagher, who had built the first church in 1860, blessed the church. Father Gallagher had come from San Francisco for the occasion. The church was thronged for Masses at 8 and 9 o'clock. A Grand High Mass commenced at 10:30, with full choir and orchestra. By this time, not even standing room was available anywhere within the church. Bishop O'Connell officiated, assisted by Fathers Manogue and Coleman of St. Mary's, Father Hugh Gallagher, Father Nulty of Gold Hill, Father Maher, and Father Tormey from Carson City.

The dedicatory sermon was preached by the Jesuit Missionary Father James Bouchard of St. Ignatius Church, San Francisco. Father Bouchard's sermon was described as being quite lengthy but was "listened to with the closest interest throughout," reported the *Virginia Evening Chronicle*. He spoke on the authority and world-wide presence of the Roman Catholic church, taking his text from St. Matthew.

"Go ye therefore, and teach all nations, baptizing them in the name of the Father, and of the Son, and of the Holy Ghost, teaching them to observe all things whatsoever I have commanded you; and lo, I am with you always, even unto the end of the world…Go where one might, among the savages of Africa and America, or among the most highly cultivated peoples of the world, the same church would be found…that we find here today in this beautiful church…"

Father Bouchard concluded with a tribute to the tireless energy and zeal of Father Manogue, ending his sermon with the words, "Father Manogue has here built for himself a monument which I hope might be as enduring as the mountains which surround it."

The Eloquent Indian

Father James Bouchard, S.J.

Father James Bouchard, S.J. was the dedicatory speaker at St. Mary's on September 16, 1877. Father John McGloin in his biography *The Eloquent Indian* relates that Father Bouchard's maternal grandparents were captured in a Comanche raid and roasted at the stake. His mother, then only seven years of age was adopted by the tribe. She was later married to a Delaware Indian chieftain. From this union was born Father Bouchard, who was called "Watomika" or "Swift Foot." He lived for 12 years as a Delaware Indian on their tribal reserves in Kansas and was introduced to the white civilization by a Presbyterian minister. He ultimately became the first American Indian to be ordained as a priest within the United States. He was known for his eloquence among the cities and mining camps of the West, and had received a special Papal dispensation to wear a long beard to protect his throat. He had lectured many times on the Comstock, starting in 1865 with a mission preached in Gold Hill and a fund raising lecture for the Daughters of Charity. His final mission or series of lectures was preached at St. Mary's in June of 1889, and he died in December of that year, at 66 years of age. He often used his Indian name of Watomika, S.J.

A view of the main altar from the old choir loft as the church appeared from 1877 to 1957.

Bishop Eugene O'Connell, Bishop of the old diocese of Grass Valley dedicated St. Mary's in the Mountains on September 16, 1877.

VIII
Paiute Parishioners

Civilization, as the white men know it, was thrust on the Paiute Indians with the hordes of silver seekers who rushed into the region from 1859. By the 1870's, the Paiutes in and around Virginia City lived in "wickiups" made of willow poles and castoffs from the white society, so that Virginia City appeared to be skirted by rows of beehives. After the fire of 1875, the "wickiups" were made more durable, with discarded gas pipes replacing the willow poles. The Indians were reduced to sawing wood and washing clothes for their white brethren, commencing a long attempt at assimilation into the white society that had inundated them. While the rest of society kept them on the fringes, Father Manogue recognized their equality before God, and many were converted to the faith by his efforts.

One well known couple, in the years before the Fire of 1875, were "Adam" and "Eve," both well advanced in years. Old Adam and Eve seemed to have embraced the Christian religion in the early days of the California Missions, and Adam was fond of being in St. Mary's and was never happier than when he conversed with Father Manogue on religious subjects. Their grandchildren were baptized by Father Manogue, and names of "Patrick" and "Michael" were

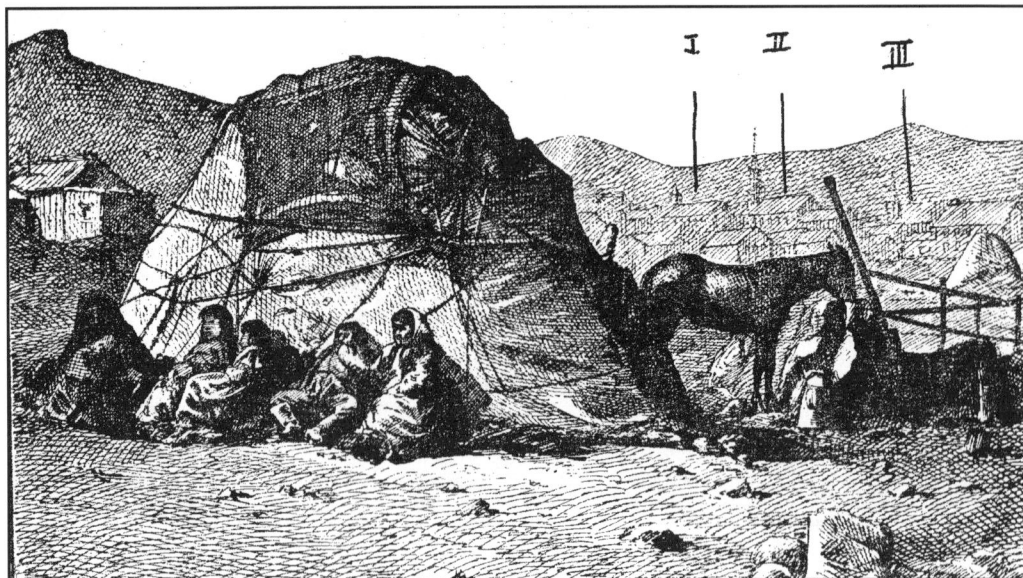

The engraving above, taken from an original photograph, was published in The Big Bonanza *by Dan de Quille. It depicts a Paiute wickiup just before the Great Fire of 1875. In the background can be seen the Methodist Church (I), the pre-fire brick St. Mary's Church (II), and St. Paul's Episcopal church behind St. Mary's (III).*

now heard in the Paiute tribe. The couple were both bitten by stray ferocious dogs, within a week of each other, and after lingering for some time under the care of the Daughters of Charity, their souls were released to the happy hunting grounds.

Captain Bob, son of Adam and Eve, reigned as Chief of the Paiutes of Storey County until his death in 1879. Because of his rank, the County Commissioners supplied him with materials to build a small shack; he literally died from a stroke of civilization, as, having been used to the cold blasts that sweep through the sagebrush, the new enclosure, with its stove, brought about his death, probably through tuberculosis. He breathed his last on February 16, 1879, surrounded by squaws who filled the air with lamentations. At his death, Father Manogue was seen coming down the hill at a long, striding clip, his cassock flying, and his hands full of the necessary sacred symbols of the last rites. The next morning, his body lay in state in St. Mary's church; all day the Paiutes crowded the sanctuary and gazed upon their dead chief, who was lying amidst burning tapers—a group of savages in red blankets and paint standing before the blue and gold Gothic Altar. The procession went forth to the cemetery that evening… "An honest and kind heart beat in the breast of the unlettered savage, and in the middle of a mad race for wealth, he lived content with what he had—an extra mule or the possession of a cast off pair of pants being the only ambition which ever tried his soul…"

The Gothic altar as it appeared in 1879, the year of the funeral of "Captain Bob," chief of the Storey County Paiutes. (C.E. Watkins photo, San Francisco).

IX

Boom Days on the Comstock 1864-1897

The Daughters of Charity

By 1864, "Virginia City was full-grown, rejoicing in life," according to *Thompson and West's History of Nevada*. By 1866, the mines were yielding over 15 million in bullion per year, and the yield from the Consolidated Virginia Mine along between 1873 and 1876 exceeded 39 million. Amidst dispatches about the Civil War, the *Virginia Daily Union* reported that the Daughters of Charity would open their school on October 17, 1864. By 1880, 400 students were in attendance, under Sister Frederica McGrath, Superioress. These were glorious days on the Comstock, and Father Manogue said that if someone was willing to supply enough of it, he would see that champagne sprayed from the water jets on the church spire for the Fourth of July of 1878. In addition, Mrs. John Mackay presented suitable grounds for a hospital, obtaining the same from the Estate of Major Van Bokkelin, who had blown himself and several other occupants of a rooming house up after he had stored dynamite and other mining supplies under his bed. The hospital, also staffed by the Daughters of Charity, was dedicated with due pomp and ceremony by Bishop O'Connell and Father Manogue in 1875. From 1865 to

1880, the parish numbered between 3000 and 5000 souls, mostly Irish miners and their families, and the days when the parish numbered between 3000 and 5000 souls, mostly Irish miners and their families, and the days when the parish could support a school and hospital can be right-

A Statue showing the Daughters of Charity as they appeared during the time the order served St. Mary's is shown above. Until recently, the same order was in charge of St. Teresa of Avila School in Carson City, where the statue occupies a prominent place in the front entrance.

fully defined as the "boom days" of the Comstock Lode. Parish fund raising efforts give reports of the auctioning of solid silver bricks and large needle-point portraits of George Washington, made painstakingly by the sisters. On one occasion, the students of St. Mary's school for girls presented a solid silver brick to a favorite music teacher.

In 1887, over 1000 parishioners jammed the school on "H" street to hear the St. Mary's Dramatic Club present the Irish Patriotic Play *Robert Emmet*, accompanied by the Virginia orchestra. On May 4, 1893, Sister Mary Angelica Olivas died in Virginia City after a prolonged illness. She had the care of the orphans of the school and was much beloved by all, and a large procession carried her to rest in the Virginia City cemetery. By 1897, the decline in mining resulted in the closing of the school and the hospital was left in the hands of secular ladies. Father Patrick Hennebery, a missionary priest who had conducted many missions at St. Mary's, died at the hospital shortly after the departure of the Sisters, and was buried next to Sister Olivas. These events mark the beginning of the long decline in the affairs of St. Mary's though undoubtedly it was not perceptible at the time, since the hope of new discoveries had always held sway among the populace of the Comstock. History was revived when the Daughters of Charity returned to neighboring Carson City to open a new school in 1957. The Sisters considered this a return to Nevada.

Virginia City in 1878, showing the newly reconstructed church (I), the Daughters of Charity hospital (II), and school and orphanage (III).

LEFT PAGE: *This photograph from St. Mary's archives shows the Daughters of Charity Hospital as it appeared around the 1870's. The photograph is taken from the East, showing the laundry building to the rear, with rows of bedsheets hanging out to dry. The mine dumps and the smoke stacks of the booming mines can be seen, as well as miners' boarding houses and other buildings, as one looks over the ridge toward Gold Hill. In the foreground is a huge stack of cordwood—the principal source of fuel on the Comstock during the boom days.*

BELOW: *Daughters of Charity school.*

X

Saint Mary's and the V & T Railroad

· ·

From the time of its construction in 1869 until its abandonment in 1938, the Virginia & Truckee Railroad, which is now fondly remembered by rail fans as one of the most famous of all shortlines, must have been a test of endurance for St. Mary's Church. In the beginning, it terminated about one block south of the church. Yet, it became the center of tragedy when the *Territorial Enterprise* reported on February 15, 1870, that James Manogue, a Comstock miner and brother to Patrick Manogue, was fatally injured when the cars of a construction train passed over his legs. He had been riding on a flat car of the train, and fell down onto the track. He was carried in a litter to his brother's church, the first wooden St. Mary's. For some time, he spoke in a strong voice, but under the primitive circumstances of the time, nothing could be done, and he expired. The following day, a funeral was held from Father Manogue's first wooden St. Mary's church.

In 1871, the railroad was extended to the center of town by the only feasible route—a tunnel directly under the immediate front of St. Mary's church. The vibration of the passing trains could be felt in church, and after the Great Fire of 1875, Father Manogue added three brick porches to the front to strengthen the structure. During the boom years of the 1870's, forty to fifty trains passed through the tunnel every day. Through its portals passed all of the commerce of the Comstock, as well as many famous figures of the day—U.S. Grant, Rutherford B. Hayes, Thomas Edison, General Sherman, Edwin Booth, and many others. It saw the comings and goings of Bishop O'Connell, the Daughters of Charity, the missionaries and religious who had occasion to visit St. Mary's. By the time Herbert Hoover passed through its portals in April 1933, less than 500 residents remained where once there had been 30,000. The railroad author Gilbert Kneiss stated that the last train in 1938 was an "empty train leaving a deserted depot in a silent town." After abandonment of the railroad, the tunnel continued to be a hazard for several years as it slowly collapsed, probably contributing to the further deterioration of the church. After many complaints about the hazard, the tunnel was finally filled in in the 1940's. In July 1976, a portion of the V & T from the old South End Depot destination to a tunnel in Gold Hill again became operational as a tourist attraction, so that today, during the summer months, the sound of a steam locomotive once again echoes through the redwood columns of St. Mary's occasionally interrupting a sermon, as it brings to life memories of such probable occurrences during the boom days.

The "E" Street Tunnel in front of St. Mary's, and a V & T special train, headed by Locomotive No. 11, the classic "Reno" emerging from the tunnel in April 1933, with U.S. President Herbert Hoover in the fireman's seat.

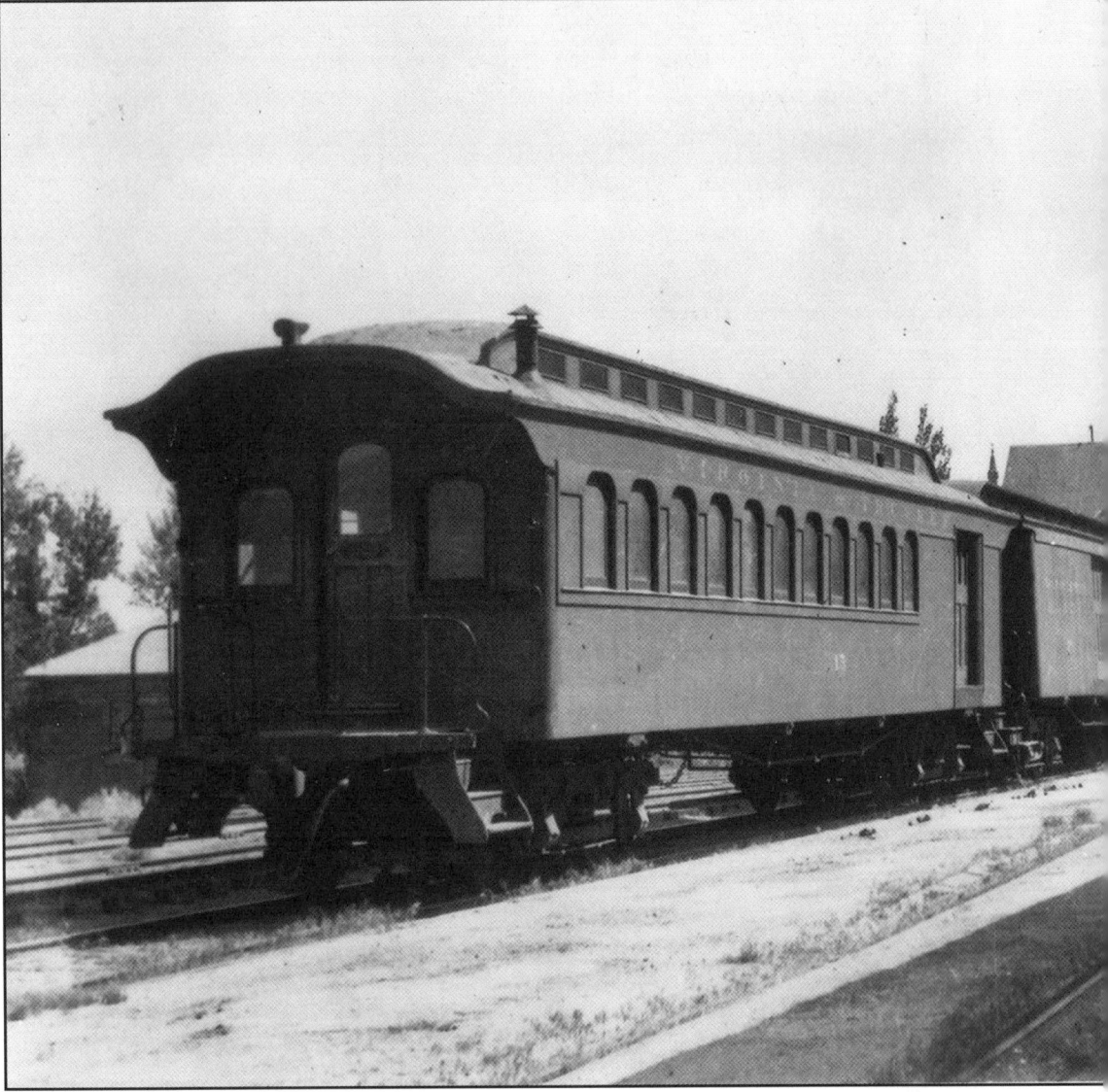

On a bright Saturday afternoon in May of 1937, the weekly steam train of the V & T Railroad "left a deserted depot in a silent town" as it swung toward the "E" street tunnel and St. Mary's church, enroute to Carson City and its connection with the Southern Pacific in Reno. (Taken from "Bonanza Railroads" by Gilbert Kneiss)

31

XI
The Long Decline

In the 1890s, silent mines and abandoned buildings began to spread on the Comstock landscape. On the somber Monday morning of March 4, 1895, the Gothic altar of St. Mary's was draped in black for a Requiem Mass for the repose of the soul of Bishop Manogue who had died a few days previously in Sacramento. Flowers on his casket were provided by Mrs. James G. Fair, widow of the Bonanza King. A representative group from Virginia City attended the funeral. On September 7, 1897, Sister Rose and Sister Regina, the last of the Daughters of Charity on the Comstock, boarded the V & T for their final departure through the tunnel that fronted the church, a church which the Order had served for 33 years. In a larger sense, these events signaled the beginning of the long decline.

Dr. Wilbur Shepperson, in his book on Nevada immigrants, *Restless Strangers,* reported that Father Daniel Murphy, fresh from Ireland, arrived at dusk on February 1, 1907, at the depot in Virginia City. The newly appointed pastor, descending from the train, "…saw buildings hanging on the side of a hill; they were in need of paint and repair. It was cold, bleak, and depressing. I thought I had come to the end of the world." In 1911, the neighboring parish of St. Patrick's in Gold Hill was closed as a parish and reduced to a mission of St.

Mary's. St. Patrick's church itself was finally dismantled for the lumber in 1918 and the contents removed to St. Mary's. Through the 1920s and '30s, St. Mary's continued to serve a slowly diminishing number of parishioners, often under the care of non-resident administrators. Mining revived a little in the 1930s with the advent of open pit excavating and the ability to process lower grade ores, so that the Comstock mines were never completely abandoned.

On June 1, 1935, a full-time pastor was again appointed during the enthusiasm caused by the Diamond Jubilee of the Catholic Church in Nevada, but again parish activities dwindled during the late 1930s and early '40s. The parishioners were reduced to a handful of people who carried bravely on. Vada Greenhalgh, Alice Byrne, Mamie Devney, Mollie Croker, Marcella Goodman, Gertrude Clouartre, the Muckles, Giraudos, Giuffras, Gallaghers, Marks and Zalac families just about constituting the whole parish roster. By this time services were held in a basement chapel during the winter, as the cost of heating the main church during this season was prohibitive for so few people. Occasionally a visitor would ask to see the interior of the main church, and Lois Murphy would serve as tour guide. These early visitors were the fore-runners of the many who would follow, seeking the remnants of the Old West and bringing the long parish decline to an end. Taking advantage of an increasing interest in the history of Virginia City, Mgr. Robert Harrigan established a small museum in the church basement. On Christmas and other special days a group of musicians would bring their instruments up to the old choir loft and accompany St. Mary's choir in one of the old Latin masses. It began to appear that, like the community itself, the future of St. Mary's depended on its historic past.

"Towering O'er the Wrecks of Time…"

In the 1930s, St. Mary's was surrounded by a city in deep depression. Lucius Beebe, in his book *The Saga of Wells Fargo*, stated that "As the timbers of the vast subterranean stopes and winzes in the abandoned mines crumbled from the earth's pressure, entire structures in Virginia City commenced to tumble down…while still remained to view the towering spire of St. Mary's in the Mountains, an allegory to who will read it as such of the enduring qualities of the Church of Rome, quite literally towering o'er the wrecks of time."

XII
Echoes of the Old Days

In the 1930s, St. Mary's essentially unchanged since its reconstruction in 1877, towered over a city slowly crumbling around it. On September 8, 1935, 1500 of the Faith met on the Comstock for the Diamond Jubilee of the Catholic Church in Nevada. At 11 a.m., the bell was tolled 48 times, and then an assemblage including two Archbishops and eleven Bishops entered the church for a solemn Pontifical Mass, accompanied by numerous priests and religious, as the combined choirs of St. Mary's and the Reno Cathedral sang, *"Ecce Sacerdos Magnus."* Six hundred people crowded the old pews, and hundreds more swarmed over the old balconies and choir loft, while yet others stood outside. The Mass was celebrated by Archbishop Mitty of San Francisco, who had received the Palium only a few days previously. Then, Robert J. Armstrong, successor to Bishop Manogue as Bishop of Sacramento, delivered the Diamond Jubilee sermon, saying, "Today there is desolation on this mountain; places once held dear are valueless. To us it is dear as the cradle of our faith." For a brief moment, pioneers on crutches and canes, the last survivors of the Irish miners, observed a glorious reawakening of old St. Mary's in the Mountains.

The slowly beating pulse quickened again for a brief time on July 28, 1939, when a bronze plaque commemorating Father Manogue was presented to the parish by his nephew, Judge Maurice T. Dooling. A monument built of Comstock mineral specimens was erected on the front porch to receive the plaque. Dr. George H. Ross, last physician of the soon-to-close County Hospital, which occupied the former Daughters of Charity hospital building, introduced Judge Dooling and the Governor of Nevada, E.P. Carville, following a High Mass celebrated by Bishop Thomas Gorman, first Bishop of Reno. By this time, the church itself was showing the marks of time, with years of deferred maintenance. Would the church crumble with the rest of the city? There was a glimmer of hope for the future as

Diamond Jubilee Pontifical Mass, September 8, 1935.

34

directly across the street had been built a new public school as a W.P.A. project—a modern building in a vast sea of old and deserted structures built during the bonanza days, recalling a few years of extreme prosperity and a long decline.

Nevada Governor E.P. Carville addresses the crowd gathered to dedicate the bronze plaque and monument to Father Manogue on July 28, 1939.

Bishop Gorman arrives at St. Mary's, July 28, 1939.

Bishop Thomas K. Gorman, first Bishop of Reno, addresses the gathering at St. Mary's in the Mountains July 28, 1939. The rock monument was later removed and the plaque affixed directly to the front wall of the church.

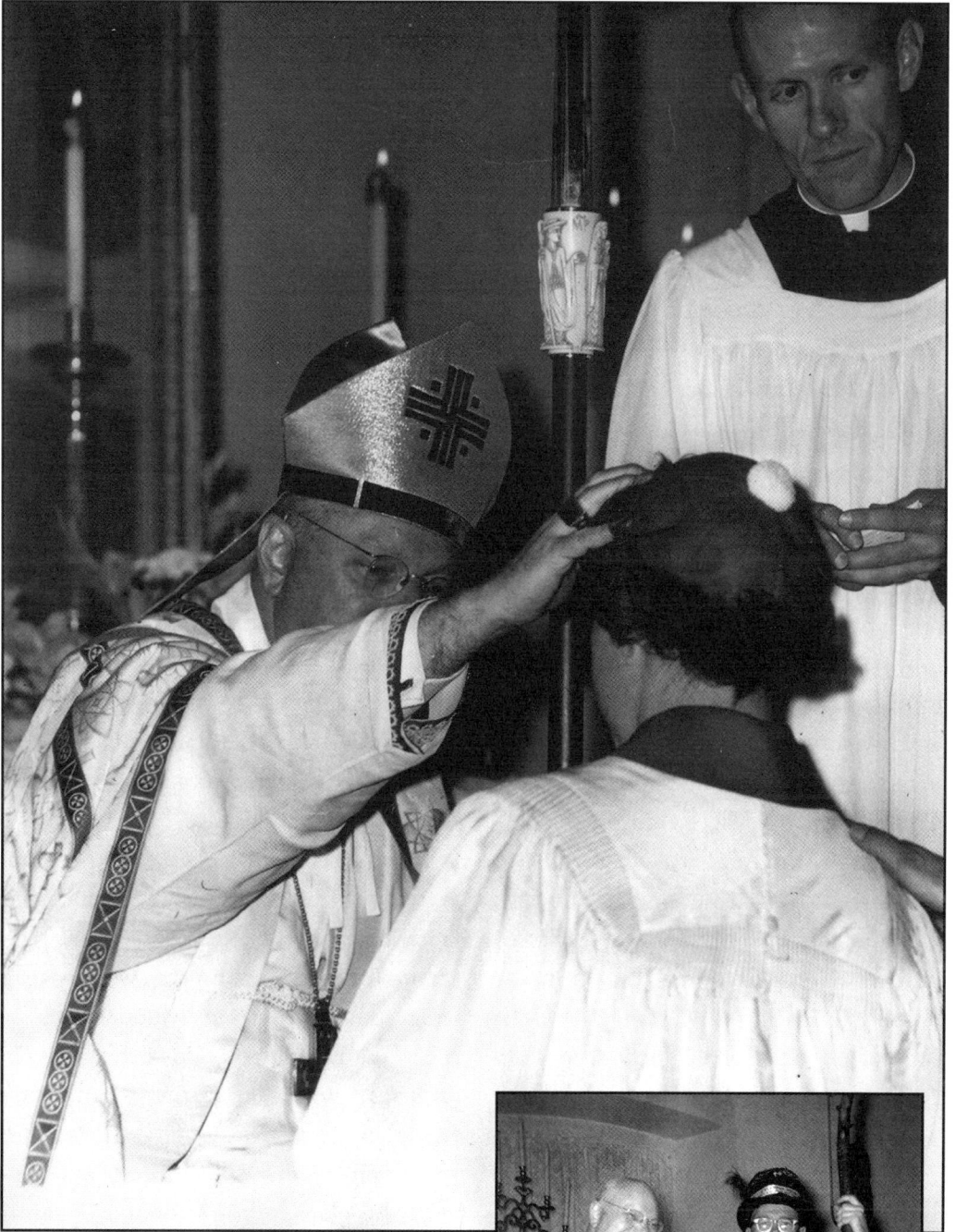

Bishop Robert J. Dwyer administers Confirmation at St. Mary's, with Father Caesar Caviglia assisting. The inset photo shows Bishop Dwyer with a high official of the Ancient Order of E Clampus Vitus, a fraternal group founded by the miners of the Old West and revived in recent times.

XIII
Borrasca

By 1940, settling of the underground tunnels had caused the brick minarets of St. Mary's to lean precariously. A leaking roof had caused much damage to the interior ceiling and walls. The south wall was beginning to pull away from the choir loft, so that a large portion of the loft had to be roped off. Bishop Gorman replaced the minarets with metal caps and removed much of the exterior ornamentation, now in a state of decay. Growing numbers of tourists were coming in to see the church, as it had survived as one of the few remaining relics of the boom days. On March 23, 1940, film actress May Robinson, on location to film "Virginia City," stopped by for refreshments served by the Altar Society. On June 9, 1943, Eleanor Roosevelt visited the Crystal Bar, St. Mary's in the Mountains, and Piper's Opera House. The interior of the church, unchanged since 1877, remained in a state of genteel decay.

On August 23, 1957, the *Territorial Enterprise* wrote a letter of inquiry to Bishop Robert J. Dwyer, then serving as the second Bishop of Reno, concerning rumors that the interior of the old church was to be modernized. The Bishop replied that "nothing of real historical value would be removed—Our aim is simply to restore and maintain its primary function as a house of God and not a museum of doubt-ful authenticity." To this end, Father Robert Jelliffe was assigned to St. Mary's. Father Jelliffe had previously formed a monastic group called the Damascus Foundation and was a proponent of new religious art forms. The Damascus Foundation had created contemporary art works for churches throughout the country. Unfortunately, Father Jelliffe, a Cistercian monk, regarded the Victorian fixtures of St. Mary's as excessively sentimental. His plans to modernize the interior of the church clashed directly with the wishes of "the most backward-looking community in Christendom" the San Francisco *Chronicle* reported. As a part of his renovation program, Father Jelliffe removed the interior fixtures of St. Mary's, and then removed the choir loft. Opposition formed in the community under the leadership of Lucius Beebe, owner of the *Territorial Enterprise.* A storm of controversy raged in the area press and in the saloons of the city. Father Jelliffe, unable to complete his plans for the interior, reluctantly concluded that the Damascus Foundation had been misplaced in its setting.

Bishop Dwyer, returning from a tour of Europe, then assigned Father Caesar Caviglia to the parish. Father Caviglia, an "old time" parish priest, was more compatible with the "backward-looking" community of Virginia

In 1940 the brick minarets were removed as safety hazards and cables were attached to the spire for removal of the old water system and for repair work to the steeple and cross.

City, whose Catholic parishioners were described in the San Francisco *Chronicle* as "a small and intractable group." Father Caviglia undertook the task of restoring structural stability to the church, whose walls were in danger of collapsing as a result of removing the choir loft. Funded by Bishop Dwyer at a cost of $33,000, nine tons of steel beams and 350 tons of concrete were used to shore up the old building, with Wallace Robenstein as architect and Jim Johnson and Marco Bostovich as contractors. This period remains fresh in the minds of the parishioners as a traumatic episode that resulted in the destruction of the interior of their beloved St. Mary's. Ironically enough, however, these events later proved to be a "saving grace" for the church. In 1980, when the Fleischmann Foundation awarded a grant to restore the exterior brickwork and roof, no structural renovations were necessary, and this was a deciding factor in the award of the grant.

In an Old Babylon, a New Jerusalem

STAINED GLASS window created under his direction for a church in Minnesota is examined by Father Robert Jelliffe, leader of dedicated band of craftsmen in Virginia City, Nev. He's an outspoken foe of "altar gingerbread" and "lace-curtain altar cloths."

THE CHURCH of St. Mary's in the Mountains appears in center of this scene of part of Virginia City, Nev. There lay artist-craftsmen organized by Father Robert work to modernize churches' art.

When the newspapers reported that the Damascus Foundation had been established in Virginia City, the stage was set for the inevitable clash between the most forward-looking artisans and "the most backward-looking community in Christendom."

As the removal of the interior fixtures continued under a "modernization program," the Territorial Enterprise *published a sketch in parody of the "modern" point of view. The editor recalled fond memories of the old Gothic interior, and the controversy continued in the press and in the saloons along 'C' Street.*

BOB RICHARDS

TOURIST OF THE WEEK

BOB RICHARDS

"Why, an antique eyesore like that is an INSULT to modern Christian dynamism!"

XIV
Hopes of Restoration

• •

By 1961, the church had been structurally renovated, but the interior was stark in appearance. A simplified main altar held the old painting of "Mary in the Mountains of Judea," and except for the redwood columns, there was little left of the original interior. Parishioners wistfully recalled its original appearance.

On May 15, 1963, Father Paul Meinecke, an admitted Comstock history buff, was assigned to St. Mary's. He cleaned and restored many of Virginia City's cemeteries with prison labor, and opened an art gallery in the church basement as a source of parish revenue. The grand opening of the art gallery was held June 21, 1964, with noted Virginia City artist Cal Bromund in attendance, and Mrs. Louise Curran as director. Many artists displayed their work in this gallery for many years.

On June 21, 1964, Cal and Mae Bromund and Father Paul Meinecke posed before a Bromund painting of St. Mary's with a young artist at the opening of the Art Gallery in the basement of the church.

In 1967, Bishop Joseph Green, successor to Bishop Dwyer, authorized Father Meinecke to restore the church as much as possible to its former condition. Unfortunately, he could provide "precious little funding." An example of Father Meinecke's ingenuity for fund-raising occurred on August 10, 1968, when the composer, Ferde Groffe, a native of Saxony, came to Virginia City. Mr. Groffe had composed the *Grand Canyon Suite* in 1931 for Paul Whiteman's Orchestra and when his son happened to meet Father Meinecke in Virginia City, arrangements were made to perform his new work, *Requiem for a Ghost Town* in Virginia City. Over 2,000 people attended as 50 musicians performed the new work in the center of town. John Carrico of the University of Nevada music department conducted the work. On the following Tuesday, a special

Centennial Mass was celebrated by Bishop Green, Bishop Alden Bell of Sacramento, and Bishop Hugh Donohue of Stockton. The Masonic Order of Knights Templars joined with the Knights of Columbus in the ceremony, in a unique gesture of ecumenism. These events were held in commemoration of the laying of the cornerstone of the first brick church in 1868.

With such an auspicious start, Father Meinecke embarked on a program to install new stained glass windows. The first of many new windows was installed in November, 1968, at a cost of $11,280. Before 1957, the church had contained only four stained glass windows and a "painted" rose window, all removed during the monastic period and replaced with plain glass. Thus Father Meinecke stated that the work was a continuation of a project never completed. Fa-

COLLECTION OF FATHER PAUL MEINECKE

Some of the 2,000 people in attendance at the concert performance of "requiem for a Ghost Town" in downtown Virginia City.

ther Meinecke awarded the window project to the Hauser Company of Winona, Minnesota, who submitted a design that was as close as he could get to the design of the old windows. He then turned his efforts to opening the old Daughters of Charity hospital, now owned by Storey County and lying vacant, as a center for artists in residence, who would then display their works in the church art gallery. With "precious little funding," he was able to restore the old brick minarets in the front of the church and rebuild much of the old wooden ornamentation over the front porches, always hoping that the old church would someday regain some of its former Gothic glories.

View of 1968 Centennial Mass, showing the structural renovations of 1960, and a simplified Main Altar.

Nevada Governor Mike O'Callaghan, Bishop Joseph Green and Father Paul Meinecke during the "Rose Window" installation ceremonies, August 19, 1973.

Bishop Joseph Green and Father Paul Meinecke greeting crowds of well wishers following concert debut of "requiem for a Ghost Town" on August 10, 1968.

By 1969, Father Paul Meinecke had restored one brick minaret and much of the wooden ornamentation over the front porches.

XV
Father Paul Meinecke —"Dona ei Requiem"

• •

Father Meinecke issued an appeal for a return of the missing Gothic fixtures. Responding to his call, Mr. Gerald Harwood, Storey County building inspector, located the pieces of a Gothic confessional and reconstructed it in the church. The confessional became the first restored fixture and again resumed its place at the rear of the church. On August 19, 1973, Nevada Governor Mike O'Callaghan and Bishop Green joined Father Meinecke in special ceremonies marking completion of the new "Rose Window" below the church belfry. On this occasion, Mr. and Mrs. Jack White, owners of the House of Memories Museum, which was the repository of many of the old fixtures, graciously returned the needlepoint portrait of the Blessed Mother made by the Daughters of Charity. It was reinstalled over the front door, where it had been for eighty years until its removal during the monastic period.

Despite an amputated leg occasioned by a rare blood disease, Father Meinecke continued to take a personal hand in restoration efforts. In May of 1974, he was engaged in restoring the front porch of the old Daughters of Charity hospital build-

BY VIRGIL BUCCHIANERI

Father Paul Meinecke, 1907-1974.

ing, now his beloved art center. Handling the huge 12" x 12" timbers brought on an aggravation of his affliction, which led to his tragic death in his quarters in the church basement on May 16, 1974. A saddened parish attended a funeral mass concelebrated by most of the clergy of the Diocese, and he was laid to rest in the Catholic cemetery in Virginia City, next to the missionary Father Patrick Hennebery and Sister Mary Angelica Olivas of the Daughters of Charity.

Exterior restoration of St. Mary's, following a grant from the Fleischmann Foundation in 1980.

XVI
A Return to Former Gothic Glories

· ·

The window project was carried on by succeeding pastors and completed at a total cost of $52,840. On December 5, 1978, a Mass of Thanksgiving was celebrated at St. Mary's. Father John Myhan, last Irish pastor of the parish, and Bishop Norman McFarland, successor to Bishop Green and a man of gigantic stature reminiscent of Bishop Manogue, entered the church in solemn procession to the strains of "All Hail to St. Patrick!" Prominently displayed at the altar was a large needle-point portrait of St. Patrick, made during the boom days by the Daughters of Charity and a gift to the church on this occasion. The portrait had been in the possession of the Dominican Sisters of Saint Mary's Hospital in Reno for many years. The Sisters graciously returned it to Virginia City and St. Mary's in the Mountains where it occupies a prominent place in the old church as a reminder of its Irish heritage.

In 1979, Angelo Petrini, owner of the Delta Saloon, headed a drive to restore the main Gothic altar. Working for many months in that year, Jim Warren, a Virginia City craftsman, completed the altar at a cost of $15,225. Father Myhan than had specifications drawn for a complete interior and exterior restoration by the Plant Brothers, a San Francisco construction firm. Under Father Myhan, the wistful wishes of his small and intractable group of parishioners began to be realized.

The guardian angel of the church again helped St. Mary's with the assignment to the parish of Father Charles Bengel. The oldest active priest in the diocese, Father Bengel had been involved in previous restoration efforts in Austin Nevada. Urging the restoration program forward, Father Bengal returned the old brass candlesticks to the main altar. Mr. and Mr. Jack White returned the old altar angels and interior gas fixtures, and these were reinstalled high on the walls and redwood pillars of St. Mary's.

In 1980, the Max C. Fleischmann Foundation awarded a grant of $180,000 to restore the exterior brickwork, and at Father Bengel's insistence a metal roof duplicating the 1877 roof was installed, the work being undertaken by the QD Construction Company of Reno. On October 1, 1981, the Robert Z. Hawkins Foundation, a foundation with close ties to the Bonanza King John Mackay, awarded a $20,000 grant to continue interior restoration. An interior stained glass arch window was built by Howard Bennett and interior doors filled with leaded glass made by Susan Del Morris were installed.

Insisting that such a beautiful church should have a pipe organ, Father Bengel hired Robert Arie Miller, a specialist in such projects, to rebuild a pipe organ constructed by William Schuelke in 1898. Cabinet makers were engaged to restore the woodwork, and make matching chimes. In 1983 the Herman family installed Victorian-style carpeting throughout the church. Fluorescent lights installed during the 1950s were removed and replaced with antique-style shaded light bulbs. Ornate front pew pillars and kneeling rails have been returned after being located in the basement of the Daughters of Charity hospital, placed there during the monastic period. In 1984, most of the old fixtures and paintings removed during the monastic period were returned to the church. Brought out of borrasca through 25 years of restoration efforts, the spire of St. Mary's still stands high over departed Comstock glories, "towering o'er the wrecks of time…"

In 1986, J.R. Wunderle, church sexton, Father Charles Bengel, pastor and Virgil A. Bucchianeri stood before the altar restored through Mr. Angelo Petrini, owner of the Delta Saloon and a prominent member of the parish.

Epilogue

St. Mary's, like Virginia City itself, is a place of memories, and a haven for old things. On a summer Sunday Morning, Father Bernard Michalik rings Father Manogue's old bell to call parishioners to Mass. Some early-arriving tourists also fill the old redwood pews and the choir sings mostly the "good old" hymns, now out of vogue in many parishes. In the next few hours, hundreds of tourists will come through the door to view a Catholic church, not of the Middle Ages or the Renaissance, but of the days of their parents. If the viewers are of an older generation, then it recalls the church of their youth. By early afternoon, the church fills with people lighting candles, spending quiet moments in prayer, or just looking at the church built by Father Manogue and his Irish miners. The attendance dwindles after October, and when the weather turns cold, services are held in a basement chapel.

On Christmas Eve, the church returns to a brief activity. By 11:30 p.m., the choir is singing Christmas carols to a slowly-filling church. If the weather is not stormy, residents from surrounding areas come to see ghosts of their Christmases past. At midnight, the choir starts to sing one of the old Latin Masses. In the soft glow of the Christmas lights, it is easy for the mind's eye to visualize how it might have been a hundred year ago…mine owners and businessmen in frock coats occupying rented pews in the front…Irish miners in tweed suits from Roos Brothers Palace Clothing Store, together with their families seated in other pews…Daughters of Charity from the school and hospital in their distinctive large cornettes…the Emmet Guard in emerald green and gold uniforms presenting arms at the elevation of the Host…a full choir accompanied by the Virginia Orchestra playing one of the old Operatic Masses…the sounds of the mines operating at full steam twenty-four hours a day in the distance, and the V & T Railroad Lightning Express with Pullman cars carried through from San Francisco rumbling through the "E" Street tunnel into the main yards…carriage lamps lighting the way accompanied by the clip-clop of horses near the front entrance, and the yellow glow of gas street lamps at each corner…the vision quickly fades, and at the end of the service, parishioners mingle for a few minutes on the front porch and then walk out into the silent Virginia City night, with the choir heading toward the Crystal Bar, where parishioner Margaret Marks and owner of the establishment provides a little late Christmas cheer "on the house." The church returns to its Winter watch over the old mining town, awaiting Spring and the coming of the new tourist season…as a guard over the old and wonderful American frontier.

Mrs. Nevada "Vada" Greenhalgh and Robert Arie Miller before the restored pipe organ. Until the time of her death in 1985, Mrs. Greenhalgh had been organist and choir director for over 70 years. Mr. Miller restored the organ and created matching chimes.

The Mountain Shepherds
Pastors and Administrators of
Saint Mary's in the Mountains

Patrick Manogue	1862–1881	George Eagleton	1952–1954
Daniel O'Sullivan	1881–1883	James Sheehy	1954–1955
C.M. Lynch	1883–1894	Herbert A. Buel	1955–1956
Thomas Tubman	1894-1904	Charles Righini	1957
F.A. Reynolds	1904–1907	Leo McFadden	1957
Daniel B. Murphy	1907–1922	Robert Jelliffe	1957–1959
Phil O'Reilly	1922–1931	Caesar Caviglia	1959–1962
Daniel B. Murphy	1931–1933	James McNalley	1962–1963
J. O'Grady	1933–1934	Paul Meinecke	1963–1974
H.J.M. Wientjes	1935	Albert Fosselman	1974
J.J. Rowe	1935–1936	Stuart Campbell	1974–1975
John Gallagher	1937	Gerald Champlin	1975–1977
John Ryan	1937–1938	John Myhan	1977–1979
John J. Callaghan	1938-1939	Charles Bengel	1979–1986
Robert J. Harrigan	1939–1945	John McShane	1986–1990
John Smith	1945–1947	Daniel Keelan	1990–1993
Alexander Beaurant	1947	Raymond Devlin	1993
Alfred McMullen	1947	Jerry Nadine	1993
John M. Sibon	1947–1948	Donald Kelly	1993
Peter T. Fisher	1948–1949	Jim Kelly	1993
Thomas J. Connally	1949	Sam Tambourin	1994
Peter T. Fisher	1949–1950	Roger Porcella (Deacon)	1995
Florence Flahive	1950	Bernard Michalik	1996–present
Lawrence Bourrie	1950–1952		

Addendum to the Second Printing

Over ten years have elapsed since this book was first published. St. Mary's continues to tower over the old mining town of Virginia City, and since Father Bengel's time, nine more pastors and administrators have continued to administer the affairs of the parish. Under Father John McShane, the imposing steeple was again repainted and spot lights installed so that the church is now visible over the town for several hours each night. In addition, two statues were installed on the front porch, one of our Lady of Grace, during the Marian Year of 1987–1988, dedicated to Vietnam veterans, and one of St. Joseph in 1989, dedicated to the visitors of the countries of the world who come to see St. Mary's. In 1991, the International Order of Alhambra installed a large plaque designating St. Mary's as a National Historic Catholic Site. In later years, the old side altars have been restored to their original places in the Sanctuary, and a complete new heating system has been installed. In 1997, a new "front altar" was built by Gene Edwards in a design and style complimenting the historic original altar and to accommodate the current Mass rites of the church. The church basement, under Deacon Roger Porcella and Father Bernard Michalik, present pastor, has been recently completely renovated for a parish hall and meeting place. The church continues to be largely supported through the many visitors that come to Virginia City to see the remnants of the Comstock Lode, though the number of local parishioners is also slowly increasing because of population growths in nearby areas. As we approach the millennium, I hope that historic old St. Mary's in the Mountains will continue to serve the community and its visitors for many years to come.

Virgil Bucchianeri
Virginia City, Nevada
May 7, 1997